DOUBLE DELIGHT

A picture diary of Leinster Rugby's all conquering 2017-18 European
Champions Cup and Guinness PRO14 campaigns

PHOTOGRAPHS BY SPORTSFILE - WORDS BY MARCUS Ó BUACHALLA

IN ASSOCIATION WITH

Bank of Ireland

IMAGES TO SAVOUR

On behalf of Bank of Ireland, it gives me great pleasure to support this wonderful Sportsfile publication that looks back on a momentous Leinster Rugby season in the Guinness PRO14 and the Champions Cup.

A journey that began in September 2017 in Wales culminated in the joyous scenes in May 2018 in the Aviva Stadium.

As title partner of Leinster Rugby, it was a pleasure to have been there with them every step of the way. Sportsfile, as the official club photographers, were also there every step of the way. At every game, training session, media and sponsor event, Ray McManus' team captured those special moments and the commitment of the players that put on the famous blue jersey.

I would like to thank Ramsey Cardy, the club photographer, and Brendan Moran, Stephen McCarthy and all the team at Sportsfile for capturing an historic season and for producing this lovely memento of a first ever PRO14 and Champions Cup double for the club.

By purchasing this book you are supporting two wonderful charities, Leinster Rugby's charity partners the Down Syndrome Centre and MS Ireland.

To the players and the back room team led by Isa Nacewa and Leo Cullen, thank you for some fantastic days.

And to the supporters, thank you for adding such colour along the way, which comes across brilliantly through the images featured in this book.

Enjoy the book and the memories that it evokes.

Francesca McDonagh
Group Chief Executive
Bank of Ireland

The photographic team:

Brendan Moran

David Fitzgerald

Eóin Noonan

Grant Pritcher

Matt Browne

Piaras Ó Mídheach

Ramsey Cardy

Richard Huggard

Sam Barnes

Seb Daly

Stephen McCarthy

Text:

Marcus Ó Buachalla

Picture editor:

Ray McManus

Editing:

Eddie Longworth

Design:

Design Gang, Tralee

Colour reproduction:

André Corvin

Printing/Binding production:

PB Print Solutions

sports*file*
PUBLISHING

Published by:

SPORTSFILE
Patterson House, 14 South Circular Road
Portobello, Dublin 8, Ireland
www.sportsfile.com

I N SPORT, YOU SPEND MOST OF YOUR TIME LOOKING forward – planning, preparing – so it can be difficult to look back on things. However, Leinster's 2017/18 season is one we all remember for the right reasons.

It was a season that began away in Newport against Bernard Jackman's Dragons, with the team being led out by Club Captain, Isa Nacewa, and one that ended at the Aviva Stadium with the same man leading out the team for the Guinness PRO14 Final against Scarlets.

Even though he would only last 18 minutes that day, the sight of Isa on the podium lifting the trophy with his team-mates was the perfect image – the symbol of what all of us at Leinster have been working so hard to achieve.

There were twists and turns along the way – just as we had predicted! An early trip to South Africa was a

THANKS FOR THE MEMORIES

logistical eye-opener but a learning experience that we all vowed to improve from. Then the usual, difficult integration of players coming back from a Lions tour meant we were probably a little undercooked going into the European Champions Cup.

Nonetheless, we managed to get off to a good start with maximum points from our first two games before two titanic battles against Exeter when the competition restarted. The players put everything on the line in those two games and we banked another eight points.

We then moved on to confront our Interprovincial rivals – somehow coming away with three more wins – before finishing off our Champions Cup with another two wins to make it a perfect sweep to top the seeding.

Attention then turned to the Six Nations and everyone at Leinster was extremely proud of what the players achieved in capturing Ireland's only third ever Grand Slam. Who could forget Johnny's drop goal in Paris when it looked like the game was up? What a moment.

When the players regrouped after the Six Nations, everything was geared towards competing on two fronts and we had to dig deep into the squad, calling on no fewer than 55 players over the course of the two campaigns.

Having navigated our way through two more memorable days at the Aviva – against Saracens and Scarlets – we were fully focused on Bilbao and an encounter with the might of Racing 92. We had all pictured a lovely sunny day down in the north of Spain but the reality was different – a cold, wet afternoon that if anything added to the unbearable tension.

Like so many finals, it could have gone either way, but the players showed excellent composure in really difficult circumstances and conditions to come away with a famous win. The outpouring of joy at the final whistle will live long in the memory.

Our journey then took us back to Dublin where we completed the double in a free-scoring PRO14 final against Scarlets – the perfect end to a perfect season.

What a journey it was. When I look back, what I remember most is a collective effort with so many people playing a part. Of course, the players are the ones who carry out the brave and magical deeds that it takes to win rugby matches, but they have a great team backing them up.

Usually, that's as much acknowledgement as they get, but on this occasion it's my pleasure and honour to say thank you to everyone whose hard work made it a season to remember – starting with the rugby and coaching team of Stuart Lancaster, Girvan Dempsey, John Fogarty, Hugh Hogan, Emmet Farrell and John Buckley.

Thank you to our medical team of Prof John Ryan, Dr Jim McShane, Garreth Farrell, Karl Denvir, Darragh Curley, Michael Thompson, Vinny Mulvey and Chris Jones. Thank you to our performance team of Charlie Higgins, Cillian Reardon, Peter Tierney, Fearghal Kerin, Diarmaid Brennan, Joe McGinley and Daniel Davey.

Thank you to all our other Academy coaches and staff including Peter Smyth, Trevor Hogan, Noel McNamara, Simon Broughton and Eoin Smyth, who invest so much time in developing of the younger players.

Thank you to Guy Easterby, Ronan O'Donnell and the one and only Johnny O'Hagan, who are with us every step of the way, ensuring everything runs to plan and giving us the luxury of only having to focus on our own jobs. Guys, thank you so much.

Thank you to our CEO, Mick Dawson, and the Professional Game Board chaired by Frank Sowman, and to everyone back at base in UCD who provide constant support and ensure the needs of the team always come first.

Thank you to the Domestic Rugby Department for their tireless work in the clubs, schools and communities in the 12 counties in nurturing the stars of tomorrow. Our *From The Ground Up* model that develops players for our senior team would not work without you.

Thank you to our sponsors, especially our main partner Bank of Ireland, whose support off the pitch

contributes so much to our success on it.

Thank you to all involved in putting together this publication, including Bank of Ireland, Laya Healthcare and Life Style Sports – their involvement allows Leinster Rugby to donate much-needed funds to our two charity partners, MS Ireland and the Down Syndrome Centre.

Thank you to Sportsfile, especially Brendan Moran, Ramsey Cardy and Ray McManus, for capturing the essence of our double-winning season (the images are just amazing) and giving us something to look back on when we are older and greyer!

My last and biggest thank you is for the supporters who go to the time, effort and expense of following the team week in, week out.

Of all the happy memories during last season's journey, I think one (or rather two) of the most uplifting moments were the sea of blue flags and jerseys when the team bus arrived at the San Memes Stadium in Bilbao, and then a fortnight later at the Aviva Stadium. Your support meant so much to us on those two occasions and right throughout the season – thank you.

Enjoy the memories!

Leo Cullen
Leinster Rugby Head Coach

The old and the new. Isa Nacewa leads his Leinster team into battle for one last season in blue as Max Deegan gets ready for his first start in Leinster colours

1

2

3

4

5

(1) Muscles of the mighty. Cian Healy introduces himself to Cory Hill

(2) Where it all began. James Ryan may have been capped by Ireland before he made his Leinster debut but his club adventures would begin off the bench in Rodney Parade

(3) That'll do Jordan. Isa Nacewa congratulates Jordan Larmour on his first Leinster senior try on his debut

(4) Story fella? Isa Nacewa and Zane Kirchner catch up after the game as Leinster start with a convincing away performance

(5) The class of 2017. Two former St Andrew's men, Jordan Larmour and Andrew Porter, smile for the cameras - the first time two former Andrew's men had taken to the field together for Leinster

SEPTEMBER 8 – **LEINSTER 37 : 9 CARDIFF BLUES**

GUINNESS PRO14, ROUND 2, RDS ARENA (13,535)

(1) Big Dev. A special moment for Devin Toner as he leads Leinster out on the occasion of his 200th cap for the province. Toner made his debut in January 2006 against the Border Reivers

(2) Remembering one of the greats. The Leinster team applaud the late Willie Duggan, regarded as one of the finest number eights to have played the game. Duggan was capped 41 times by Ireland and toured with the British and Irish Lions to New Zealand in 1977

1

2

" I owe an awful lot to Mick Quinn. Mick and his brother Charlie Quinn, they were my senior coaches and at the end of fifth year they mentioned to me where was I going to play after school? And this was completely alien to me. It had never dawned on me that this might kick on from school into something more"

Devin Toner reflects on where it all began in Castleknock College

1   2

(1) I got this. Much to the disbelief of Scott Fardy and Josh van der Flier, Devin Toner does on his 200th cap what he's been doing since day one. He rises into the night sky to claim another lineout ball for Leinster

(2) Barry Daly, who would finish the season as the Guinness PRO14 Top Try Scorer, gets up and running for the season beating Welsh international Alex Cuthbert to the ball

2

3

(1) Try time. Nick McCarthy can't conceal his delight as he scores his first try for Leinster Rugby. He just needs to figure out how to get up now

(2) Here's lookin' at you Dev

(3) Family. Devin and Mary Toner celebrate Devin's achievement after the game

2

(1) Welcome to South Africa. Joey Carbery feels the full force of a Southern Kings welcome as his march towards the try line comes to a thundering halt. Dave Kearney is thankfully on hand to add extra ballast to push Carbery over the line for a try

(2) History made. Luke McGrath and Seán Cronin get into the action as Leinster become the first Irish club side to win a game on South African soil

SEPTEMBER 22 – **CHEETAHS 38 : 19 LEINSTER**

GUINNESS PRO14, ROUND 4, TOYOTA STADIUM (6,980)

(1) A change of scenery. James Tracy and Joey Carbery make their way towards training in Bishops College in Cape Town

(2) Down to earth. Jack Conan and the rest of the Leinster team were brought back down to earth with a bang as an early Cheetahs onslaught caught them cold. A Barry Daly hat-trick of tries couldn't rescue anything for Leo Cullen's men

1

2

1

2

3

(1) Bringing Sexto back. Johnny Sexton makes his first
appearance of the season and steers Leinster to a good
win against an improving Edinburgh side

(2) Spot the difference. Twin brothers Bryan and Ed Byrne
discuss tactics as they get ready for another set-piece

(3) Spot the ball. Nobody – least of all Jordi Murphy –
seems to know quite where the ball has gone

(4) Try as he might. Newly signed forward Scott Fardy would
have a brilliant debut season but getting up and running on
the score board took him more time than
he'd have liked

4

1

2

(1) Meep meep. The sight of a rampaging Seán Cronin taking on two Edinburgh defenders

(2) Jamison Gibson-Park scores a late try to deny Edinburgh a losing bonus point and ensure a good win over the Conference B rivals

1

2

(1) Where there is smoke. Leinster and Munster brought the fire in a hugely physical game at the Aviva Stadium with Johnny Sexton captaining the side and leading them out

(2) Bringing the roar. 12,229 supporters purchased Season Tickets for the 2017/18 season and they were there at the Aviva Stadium as they were for every other step of a momentous season

1

2

(1) Will finds a way. Despite the best efforts of Robin Copeland and CJ Stander, Rory O'Loughlin shows determination and strength to touch down for one of his two tries at the Aviva Stadium

(2) Adam Byrne slips by the attempted tackle of Munster winger Andrew Conway

(3) Johnny Sexton kicks the penalty that takes him ahead of Felipe Contepomi and on to 1,234 career points for Leinster and sets him out on his own as the province's all-time leading points scorer

3

❝ I'm delighted for Johnny. I was surprised he was turning away so many shots at goal last weekend, kicking to the corner. It was good that he had a few shots at goal today… he's going to play a huge part in our season❞

Leo Cullen reacts to Sexton's scoring record

❝ It's the one game growing up that you always wanted to watch. Of course there were semis and finals but Munster and Leinster was always the big one. Tears if you lost. Tears of joy if you won. It's the game everyone wanted to win. It still is"

Josh van der Flier discusses what makes the Leinster and Munster rivalry so special

4

(1) As Tommy O'Donnell and Robin Copeland attempt to negotiate a path over Conor Murray, Jack Conan makes the hard yards through the middle

(2) Josh van der Flier comes back for a second bite at Chris Farrell

(3) Johnny Sexton leaves the Aviva Stadium with the thanks of all those present. His son Luca isn't quite so sure what all the fuss is about

(4) Maybe he should have left it at the first bite. Josh van der Flier shows the scars of a hard-earned win over Munster

OCTOBER 14 – **LEINSTER 24 : 17 MONTPELLIER**

EUROPEAN CHAMPIONS CUP, ROUND 1, RDS ARENA (15,995)

1

(1) Joey Carbery gets Leinster's Champions Cup campaign off to a flier
with a try in the corner against Montpellier

(2) Robbie Henshaw powers through the imposing Ruan Pienaar
as he sets up another Leinster attack

OCTOBER 14 – **LEINSTER 24 : 17 MONTPELLIER**

EUROPEAN CHAMPIONS CUP, ROUND 1, RDS ARENA (15,995)

(1) One born every minute. When August Fardy decided to arrive fit and healthy into the world, it meant a reshuffle for Leinster and as Scott Fardy headed to Holles Street with his wife Penelope, James Ryan headed to the RDS for his European debut

(2) As Jack Conan gets ready to pounce, Dan Leavy rises highest into the Ballsbridge sky to claim another one of Seán Cronin's darts

1

" He was born 12 minutes before kick-off"
Scott Fardy reflects on the timing of baby August's arrival

2

2

3

(1) Leading the Charge. Jack Conan takes the fight to Montpellier's Joe Tomane as the Leinster backline gets ready to take over

(2) As Montpellier stage a second-half comeback, the Laighin Pit and the rest of the RDS come even more into play

(3) Despite some nervy second-half moments, Rhys Ruddock addresses the Leinster huddle after a job well done and a bonus point win secured

1

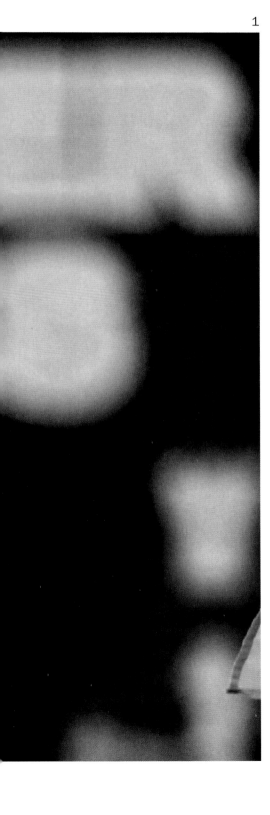

2

3

4

(1) It took a brilliant performance from captain Johnny Sexton and the rest of the Leinster players to deliver a second bonus point win on the road in Scotstoun Stadium

(2) As the rest of the Leinster players and the 7,351 supporters in Scotstoun look on, Leinster outhalf Johnny Sexton kicks a conversion

(3) Over. Under. Through. Despite the best efforts of Glasgow Warriors' Peter Horne, Dan Leavy still finds a way to get through the tackle

(4) Fergus McFadden fends off the attention of Leonardo Sarto

1

canterbury
LEINSTER
Bank of Ireland
GILBERT
FINALS 2018
McCREA

2

3

4

(1) Eat dust. Jamison Gibson-Park leaves Finn Russell in his wake
as the New Zealander sets off on another mazy run

(2) Jamison Gibson-Park and Dan Leavy are first to congratulate
inside centre Noel Reid on his first Champions Cup try

(3) As James Ryan gets set to support, Rhys Ruddock is tackled
by Callum Gibbins of Glasgow Warriors

(4) Smiles all round. And why not. It's two from two to start the Champions
Cup campaign with two try bonus points also secured

1

2

3

(1) Roll out the red carpet. The second interprovincial derby of the season was a visit to the Kingspan Stadium in Belfast

(2) Jordi Murphy stretches every sinew in his body to dispossess Alan O'Connor in the Ulster lineout

4

5

(3) Jordan who? Ulster are 3-0 up after 15 minutes then Jordan Larmour announces his arrival onto the world stage with a brilliant finish duly acknowledged by Messrs. Byrne and Gibson-Park

(4) Seán O'Brien is tackled by Sean Reidy and Kieran Treadwell of Ulster as Devin Toner and Richardt Strauss get ready for contact

(5) Sell it. Ross Byrne gives Ulster's Christian Lealiifano the eyes as he looks to step his opposite number

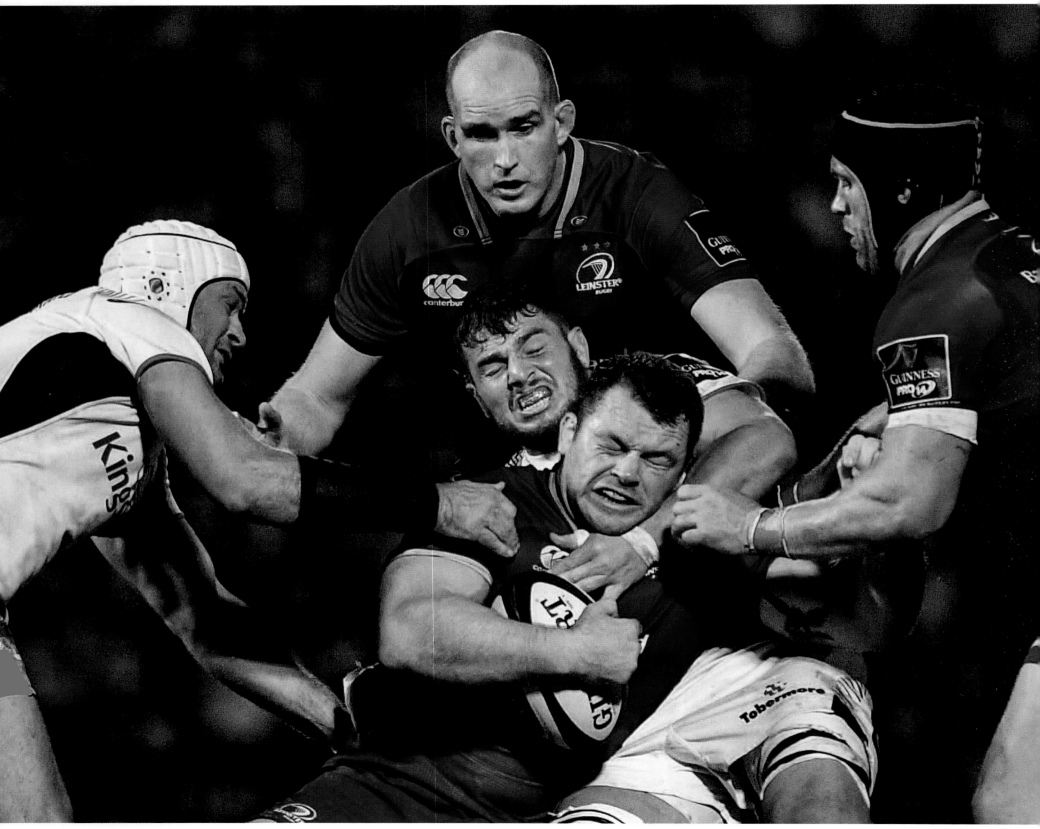

2

(1) Ulster's Seán Reidy does his best to dispossess Leinster prop Cian Healy

(2) Some legends are made there. Some are made in Tullow. Seán O'Brien leaves the field after a comprehensive win over Ulster

1

(1) Over the course of the 2017/18 season Leinster Rugby would use nine captains in total. Former St Michael's college lock Ross Molony leads Leinster out in Scotstoun Stadium in the Guinness PRO14

(2) Air Jordan. Jordan Larmour assesses his options mid-flight

1

2

3

4

(1) Jamison Gibson-Park makes things uncomfortable for his opposite number

(2) On his debut Westmeath's Conor O'Brien breaks clear of the Glasgow cover

(3) Hugo Keenan and Andrew Porter assess their options as Glasgow get set to attack again

(4) With two tacklers to contend with Leinster winger Adam Byrne does brilliantly to keep his eye on the try line as he touches down for a brilliant individual finish

(5) Fireworks in Glasgow. But on this occasion it was the home side who stole the show

5

(1) Leinster Rugby's new signing James Lowe finally lands in Dublin and, on his first trip to the RDS Arena, bumps into a few familiar faces

(2) Isa Nacewa evades Jared Rosser of the Dragons and sprints for the line to score Leinster's second try of the night

(3) Ian Nagle rises above Joe Davies to gather the lineout possession

3

1

2

3

4

(1) Over a brilliant personal season Seán Cronin would play 25 games in total for Leinster and score four tries. Here he is on a trademark burst through the heart of the Dragons defence

(2) I got you Marshy! Scott Fardy gives Leinster outhalf Cathal Marsh a helping hand as they go in search of more scores

(3) Always keep your eyes on the ball, kids. Jordi Murphy puts into practice all the things he has learned over the years

(4) Josh Murphy celebrates his first senior start for Leinster with fellow Academy player Conor O'Brien, who was also celebrating his first game at the RDS Arena

2

(1) Cometh the hour. James Lowe becomes Leinster player #1262 as he makes his debut against Benetton Rugby in the Stadio Monigo

(2) Cometh the man. James Lowe rumbles over Benetton fullback Marty Banks for one of his two tries in a Guinness Man of the Match performance that will give Leo Cullen plenty to ponder ahead of a massive few weeks of European rugby

2

3

(1) James Tracy tries to eke out the extra few yards with Scott Fardy in support

(2) In the name of the Father. Garry Ringrose prays for some divine intervention. Luke McGrath, Ross Byrne and Jack McGrath will have to do on this occasion

(3) Welcome to the family. Leinster Rugby president Niall Rynne congratulates Vakh Abdaladze on his Leinster Rugby debut

2

3

(1) Tadhg Furlong doesn't know whether he is coming or going. But one thing's for sure – Jonny Hill of the Exeter Chiefs is coming with him

(2) Waltzing Wallaby. Scott Fardy takes off with three Lions in support

(3) Jack Conan would have a number of big plays in the freezing cold of Sandy Park and more often than not it took more than one man to stop him

2

" Probably the forwards slowed down a bit and were sucking a bit of diesel towards the end, I certainly was anyway. But to go through that many phases and hold onto the ball for that long is pleasing and in the game of rugby pretty unusual. Exeter are a really tough team to stop"

Tadhg Furlong looks back on a hard earned win in Sandy Park

(1) Luke McGrath races clear of Don Armand of Exeter Chiefs. Just in case he doesn't make it, Seán O'Brien makes sure to let him know where he is

(2) When you go into a game as the underdog. But score a try with six minutes to go. After 44 phases of play. Away from home. Against the reigning Premiership champions. Where they had been unbeaten in over 12 months. This is what it means to Fergus McFadden as he reacts to Jack Conan's late try

1

2

3

4

*" **We've tried to learn from scenarios like say Clermont last year, when we've been behind. But if we trust each other on the pitch, trust the system, trust what we've done in training, hopefully we can get the result in the end"***

Garry Ringrose, after playing his part in a stunning Leinster comeback

(1) Do you remember that time? Brian O'Driscoll of BT Sport catches up with his former team-mate Seán O'Brien ahead of the return fixture against Exeter Chiefs

(2) Seán Cronin hands off Matt Kvesic of Exeter Chiefs. Note he has a full set of teeth here

5

6

(3) Even though Henry Slade is coming across and applying pressure, Leinster fullback Rob Kearney still gets his kick away

(4) Garry Ringrose looks to step Tomas Francis, who has other ideas

(5) Having been 17-3 behind at one stage, Leinster stage one of the best comebacks of the season against Exeter in the Aviva Stadium. In the 65th minute replacement Dan Leavy breaks through the Exeter cover to pop a pass to the supporting Luke McGrath

(6) Thanks Dan. Luke McGrath finishes off the move and crosses the whitewash for the only Leinster try in a pulsating game. The try puts Leinster ahead for the first time in the game and they see it home from there

2

(1) James Ryan, Dan Leavy and Scott Fardy get to Luke McGrath first to celebrate his try. It's fair to say they enjoyed the moment

(2) Not many saw that comeback from 17-3 down but the crowd of over 40,000 never gave up hope and drove the team on

1

2
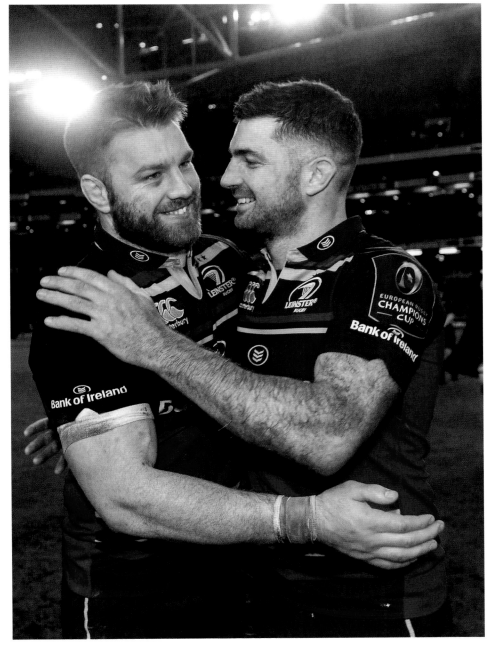

3

(1) Jack Conan and Tadhg Furlong know that that one was special. Four from four and top of Pool 3, the team had put themselves in the driving seat for the knockout stages of the Champions Cup

(2) Two warriors in blue. Seán O'Brien and Rob Kearney celebrate at the full-time whistle

(3) There's definitely no full set of teeth here for Seán Cronin but job done and a happy Limerick man

2

3

4

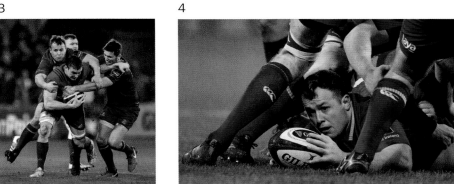

(1) When Playing Leinster – Lesson Number 375: never kick to Jordan Larmour in open space

(2) "Look at that footwork… this is the danger that he can cause… and then the pace. He has support Larmour… I told you this man was impossible to catch… Jordan Larmour with one of the most thrilling tries you will ever see." Mark Robson, *Sky Sports*

(3) Ed Byrne and Ross Byrne put a halt to Tommy O'Donnell as he looks to claw Munster back into the game

(4) Who wants it? Ed Byrne puts the ball on a plate for Jamison Gibson-Park to whip it away

1
2

(1) Jamison Gibson-Park gets a helping hand from CJ Stander of Munster as he tries to break away

(2) Despite CJ Stander's best efforts Leinster outhalf Ross Byrne still manages to get his cross field kick away

1

(1) New year. Same old Leinster. Leinster pick up where they left off in 2017 with a win against another interpro rival

(2) Not for the first or the last time, James Lowe powers through a tackle. Connacht's Tiernan O'Halloran on the receiving end of this run

2

2

3

4

(1)   Max Deegan would play a huge role in deciding the outcome of this game. In the 28th minute he crossed for Leinster's opening try and 52 minutes later he won a decisive penalty at the breakdown to deny Connacht one last shot at victory

(2)   When two nines go to war. With Six Nations squad announcements just around the corner Kieran Marmion and Luke McGrath scrap it out at the RDS

(3)   James Lowe looks to get around Connacht's Tom McCartney. He succeeds

(4)   Ross Molony celebrates Max Deegan's late intervention as Josh van der Flier dives in to congratulate Deegan

1

2

(1) 'Welcome back John'. Leinster Rugby Kicking
Coach Emmet Farrell extends a warm hand to
former Leinster player John Cooney

(2) A penny for them? Johnny Sexton walks the
pitch ahead of the final Interprovincial game of the
Christmas schedule

(3) A packed RDS welcomes Leinster and
Ulster on to the pitch

3

1

2

3

4

(1) 5 minutes. Jordan Larmour celebrates the first try of the evening at the RDS

(2) 15 minutes. Barry Daly adds another try to his personal collection as he crosses for his sixth try of the season

5

6

(3) 47 minutes. Fergus McFadden scores his first try of the season

(4) 51 minutes. Four minutes after his first, McFadden scores his second. But *this* try was all about the break from inside his won 22 by Andrew Porter who smashed his way through two Ulster players before passing to Jamison Gibson-Park who in turn fed McFadden

(5) 66 minutes. The Guinness Man of the Match Jordan Larmour pops up for his second try of the night as the game moves into the final quarter

(6) 81 minutes. Johnny Sexton has the final say, going over unopposed after another Ulster turnover and some deft touches by Jordi Murphy, Noel Reid and Max Deegan

2

3

4

(1) Yes Fardo! Scott Fardy touches down for his first Leinster Rugby try as Jordi Murphy, Dan Leavy and James Lowe celebrate the moment. Bryan Byrne in the background celebrates the try on the occasion of his own Champions Cup first; his debut

(2) 'Get at their ten Siua!' No surprises as Johnny Sexton takes the rough as he gets his pass away under pressure from Siua Halanukonuka of Glasgow Warriors

(3) With Leinster scrumhalf Jamison Gibson-Park otherwise engaged, tighthead prop Andrew Porter puts his hand up for selection

(4) Robbie Henshaw focuses on getting his pass away as Nick Grigg comes thundering in to tackle

(1) In December 2017, Jordi Murphy announced his decision to leave his home club to join Ulster Rugby for the 2018/19 season. Two months later he scores a brilliant try under the posts against Glasgow. Jordi (6) lets his emotions go and the rest of the team follow suit and let him know exactly what they think of him

(2) Bilbao Finals 2018. With a good win against the Glasgow Warriors secured, the road to Bilbao becomes clearer as Isa Nacewa addresses the players in the middle of the RDS pitch

2

❝ There's no magic formula. Everyone is working hard. There's a lot of disappointment at how we finished last season. Losing two semi-finals has a very 'almost' feel about it, doesn't it? A lot of work to get us to those semi-finals. It's nice to have a quarter-final, even if it is a couple of months away, on the horizon to look forward to"

Five wins from five games and the only 100% record in Europe, Leo Cullen is a happy man

2

3

(1) Tús maith leath na hoibre. Ross Byrne scores Leinster's first try after only four minutes in the Altrad Stadium, his first in Leinster blue. Or white

(2) Another step on the journey for young Jordan Larmour as he makes his first European start on the wing for Leinster. He was kept on his toes by Jesse Mogg but, as in all the other tests thrown his way, he more than held his own

(3) 'Would you look at the size of him?' Isa Nacewa sizes up the imposing threat of the six foot four, nearly 21 stone Montpellier winger Nemani Nadolo

2

(1) Centres of excellence. Isa Nacewa and Robbie Henshaw formed the Leinster midfield partnership for much of the European campaign, and after the Montpellier game Isa congratulates the Westmeath man on another stellar performance

(2) Job done. Leinster needed only a point from the visit to France to secure top seeding. Instead they took home four and with it a home Quarter-Final in the Champions Cup in April

FEBRUARY 9 – **EDINBURGH 29 : 24 LEINSTER**
GUINNESS PRO14, ROUND 14, MYRESIDE (3,930)

(1) 100 not out. Michael Bent joins an exclusive club of Leinster
Rugby players to have played a century of games for the club

(2) The Bull Kearney. Clontarf's Mick Kearney charges up field and
gets set to take on Rory Sutherland of Edinburgh

1 2

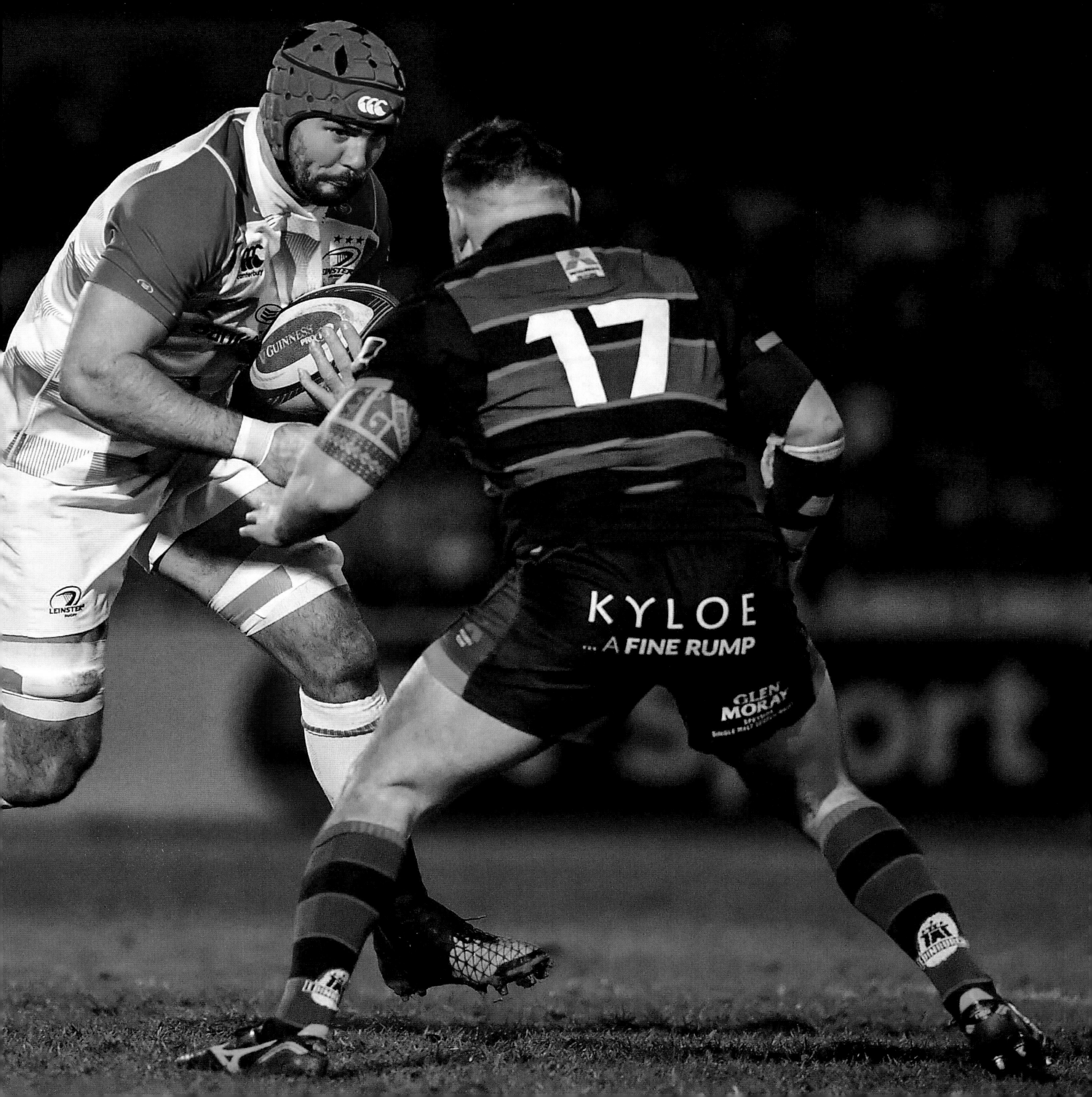
17
KYLOE
... A FINE RUMP
GLEN MORAY
GUINNESS
LEINSTER

(1) Dave Kearney is tackled by Dougie Fife of Edinburgh
as the home side go in search of a famous win

(2) Ed Byrne looks to twin brother Bryan for the answers but
sometimes there are none and it just doesn't go your way.
Despite scoring four tries and playing well for most
of the game, Leinster came up short away in Edinburgh

1

2

(1) Part one of a four-part mini-series. Wayne Pivac's Scarlets side put an end to Leinster's trophy hopes in 2017 and they would play a key part in the 2018 narrative as well. James Lowe would get to like the Scarlets too. The feeling was not mutual

(2) Peter Dooley and Richardt Strauss earn the hard yards despite the best efforts of the Scarlets pack

2

3

(1) As referee John Lacey gives it the all-clear, James Lowe celebrates his second try of the game – two by the 34th minute

(2) Max Deegan and Ian Nagle give Scott Fardy a lift as Oisín Heffernan gets set to latch on

(3) A product of Skerries Community College, Skerries RFC and the Leinster Youths pathway, Ciarán Frawley celebrates his full Leinster debut having scored two fine kicks off the bench

2

(1) Time for Leinster to return the hospitality as the Southern Kings make their first visit to Dublin and to the RDS. The hospitality didn't extend to matters onfield as Leinster ran in ten tries for a comfortable win. Ed Byrne in action against Arthur de Wee as Nick McCarthy, Josh Murphy and Mick Kearney get ready to support Byrne

(2) Should have had his porridge. Will 'Porridge' Connors slips through the attempted tackle of Andisa Ntsila of Southern Kings

1

2

❝ *They're a great club, hugely supportive of me and my career. I played all the way up to Under 18s there, a bit of AIL. They're a great club to be a part of and it's definitely on the bucket list to hopefully play a game for them again in the future"*

Ciarán Frawley acknowledges his home club Skerries RFC

(1) Ciarán Frawley takes up where he left off the week before and kicks seven conversions during a Guinness Man of the Match performance on his first start

(2) Carlow's Bryan Byrne is tackled by Anthony Volmink and Michael Willemse of Southern Kings. A good night for the young hooker as he starts the game and scores two tries

(3) Barry Daly doing what Barry Daly does. It's another two tries for the UCD winger

(4) Naas man Adam Coyle shows his delight after coming off the bench for his Leinster debut

4

1

2

1) Spot the gap. For 80 minutes all was going to plan in Parc y Scarlets. Noel Reid threads a ball in behind the Welsh club's defence

(2) But in the 81st minute Dan Jones kicks a penalty for the home side to rescue a draw from the jaws of defeat. Not a win. Not a loss. But Adam Byrne, James Lowe and Ross Byrne know that dropped points now could cost them in May

1

2

(1) A second trip to Wales in the space of a few weeks but this time Leinster come away empty handed. Rory O'Loughlin was a regular for Leo Cullen over the season but not even his try on 52 minutes could change the outcome in Swansea

(2) Only a week after their Grand Slam heroics with Ireland, Jordi Murphy and Jack McGrath carry the fight to Justin Tipuric and his pack

APRIL 1 – **LEINSTER 30 : 19 SARACENS**

EUROPEAN CHAMPIONS CUP QUARTER-FINAL, AVIVA STADIUM (51,700)

1

2

(1) And the reward for top seeding in the Champions Cup? The reigning two-time European champions Saracens coming to town. 'Bring it on' says a sold out Aviva Stadium

(2) Thanks Jamie. The Official Leinster Supporters Club make a special presentation to the retiring Jamie Heaslip who gets a standing ovation for all his efforts in the blue of Leinster

(3) First blood. Garry Ringrose scores the game's opening try after just three minutes

APRIL 1 – **LEINSTER 30 : 19 SARACENS**

EUROPEAN CHAMPIONS CUP QUARTER-FINAL, AVIVA STADIUM (51,700)

(1) Maro's the Lion. But Dan's the man. Dan Leavy evades Maro Itoje's despairing tackle to score Leinster's second try and to put daylight between the two sides

(2) Hands up! James Lowe leads the crowd – and Devin Toner – in celebration as his try after 57 minutes all but sealed Leinster's passage to the Semi-Final

1

2

❝ They're not the champions for nothing. They're a quality team. Full of internationals, both English and other nationalities. It's international rugby in all but name"

Stuart Lancaster sets the scene as Leinster take on the two-time European champions at the Aviva Stadium

(1) James Ryan claims a lineout in front of Saracens' Maro Itoje

(2) Gather around. Isa Nacewa gathers *the Brothers* in the post-match huddle, including Max Deegan who made his European debut against the reigning two-time champions

2

" Losing to Clermont last season is etched in the back of our heads"

*Isa Nacewa doesn't shy away from what has motivated the squad
to a second Champions Cup Semi-Final in two seasons*

1

2

3

(1) The smooth. Two Italian teams in two weeks to the RDS Arena. First up Zebre. Rory O'Loughlin slips by Marcello Violi

(2) How many men does it take to stop James Lowe from scoring? More than two anyway

(3) Gavin Mullin celebrates his debut with Conor O'Brien after the match

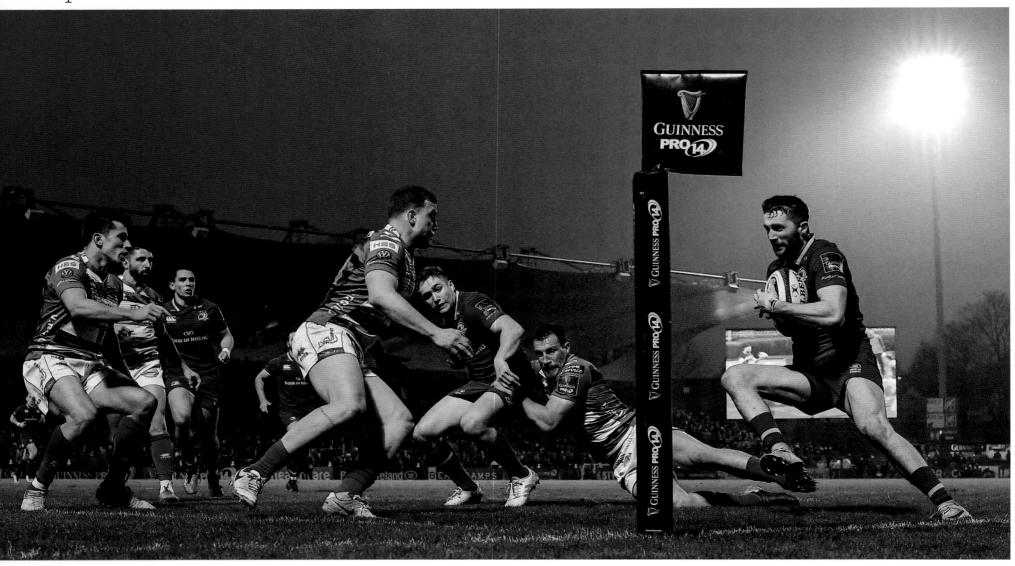

2

(1) The rough. Despite a strong Leinster start, Benetton Rugby come to the RDS to register a first win ever over Leinster at the venue. Barry Daly scores to put Leinster into a commanding 12-5 lead at the break

(2) Tommaso Iannone shows the determination that would see his side over the line as he hangs on to Adam Byrne

(3) Head scratcher. Peadar Timmins and his team-mates react at the final whistle

3

THE ONE TO W

(1) 12 county army. The men, women and children of Leinster wear their colours and show their appreciation as Isa Nacewa leads their team onto the pitch

(2) Isa Nacewa has his eyes set on one thing and one thing only

(3) And yet… still has time for a quick pic with the two Bank of Ireland Match Day Mascots, Finn Byrne (11) and Dylan Maher (7)

1

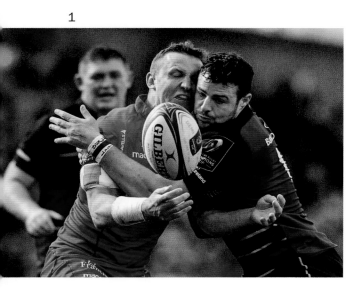

2

3

(1) No quarter given. Hadleigh Parkes and Robbie Henshaw going to the wire for their respective sides

(2) He picks his moments. James Ryan scored with his second touch as an Ireland international and now he scores his first ever Leinster try after only nine minutes in the Champions Cup Semi-Final to send Leinster on their way

(3) The agony in the ecstasy. Fergus McFadden scores Leinster's third try just before half time to send the team in at the break 24-9 ahead. McFadden though tore his hamstring in the act of scoring and with that, his season was over

2

3

(1) As Scott Fardy scores Leinster's fourth try early in the second half, the Leinster supporters in the stands start to think of planes, trains and automobiles for Bilbao

(2) Job done. Johnny Sexton scores a try to put Leinster 39-9 in front with 20 minutes to go. Scarlets would score a late consolation try but there would be no way back from there as Sexton signed off with 18 points to his name.

(3) The generation game. Isabella Gibson-Park, Finn and Cillian Cronin and Max Toner celebrate reaching a first European Champions Cup Final since 2012 with their proud fathers

1   2

3

4

(1) Noel Reid leads the team out on the occasion of his 100th cap. The former St Michael's College student made his debut in October 2011 against Aironi

(2) Friend. Foe. Ross Molony wins a line out despite the best efforts of former Leinster player and Connacht lock Gavin Thornbury

(3) Perseverance. On the 11th August 2017, Tom Daly tore his ACL in the first pre-season friendly game of the season. Nearly nine months of intensive rehabilitation later he makes his first appearance of the season in the centre

(4) 55 players were used by Leinster Rugby during the 2017/18 season. Mayo born Caelan Doris would be the last of those players to feature as he made his debut off the bench against Connacht becoming Leinster player #1268

Turning Bilbao Blue

(1) The conditions didn't make for great fare. But that didn't seem to bother James Ryan who again delivered a performance for the ages

(2) Dan Leavy is tackled by Virimi Vakatawa of Racing 92

(3) Jamison Gibson-Park is tracked and caught by Yannick Nyanga and Baptiste Chouzenoux of Racing 92

(4) Virimi Vakatawa grabs hold of whatever part of Rob Kearney that he can

2

A tale of two kickers

(1) Isa Nacewa puts boot to ball as he scores his last points in Leinster colours to bring his career tally to 706. The penalty kick put Leinster into the lead for the first time in the game in the 78th minute

(2) Two minutes later, Racing replacement Remi Tales has a drop goal to level matters with time up. James Ryan, Jack Conan and Scott Fardy have other ideas and would ensure that there would be no easy shot for Tales who forced his kick to the left and wide

1

2

(1) Nine games. Nine wins. Champions of Europe. James Ryan celebrates at the final whistle

(2) Here's Johnny! Johnny Sexton would play in seven of the nine Champions Cup games. 403 minutes in total and he would contribute four tries, 13 conversions and 11 penalties for a personal haul of 79 points. He deserved his moment

(3) As did they all...

3

(1) A family affair as Luke McGrath celebrates with his mother Michelle and sister Emma

(2) Selfie time! Rory O'Loughlin spots some familiar faces in the San Mames Stadium

(3) Isa and Johnny. 15 points between them and two medals to show for their efforts

(4) History made. Johnny Sexton, Cian Healy, Devin Toner and Isa Nacewa join French legends Cedric Heymans and Freddie Michalak as the only four-time European title winners in the history of the competition

(5) Jamison Gibson-Park confirms that it does indeed taste better from a bigger cup

5

" *Sexto and Isa spoke to us at half time and just said 'we're nearly there' so when you have leaders like that with you with that calmness to keep us in the game, it's not that hard to stay focused. It's just unbelievable that we've now done it. I'm just delighted for the whole squad, the backroom team, the supporters"*

Heineken Man of the Match James Ryan chats about the influence of Isa Nacewa and Johnny Sexton

1

2

3

4

(1) Refocus. And go again. James Lowe brings the RDS to their feet as his audacious pass out the back puts Jack Conan through for a try against Munster in the Guinness PRO14 Semi-Final

(2) Nobody enjoys winning a scrum penalty as much as Jack Conan. Apart from James Lowe

(3) Ross Byrne gets the back line moving again as the Leinster outhalf sets up another attack inside the Munster half

(4) As Munster come roaring back into the game, the Laighin Pit make their voices heard

1

2

3

4

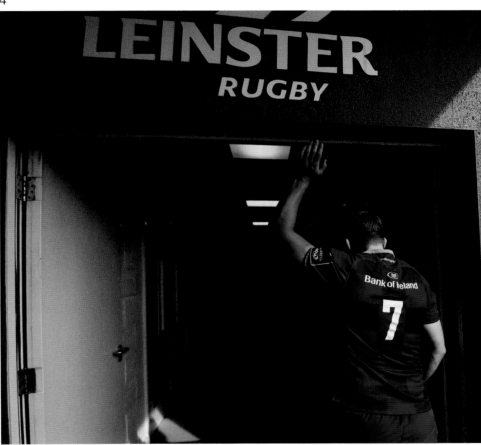

(1) Like he did on the 1st January against Connacht, Max Deegan comes to the fore with a massive moment right at the death, winning a penalty for Leinster with Munster bearing down on the line. The turnover would ultimately win Leinster the game and a spot in the Guinness PRO14 Final

(2) Cian Healy and Devin Toner ensure that James Ryan gets to the ball ahead of Munster's Peter O'Mahony

(3) Isa Nacewa takes the applause of team-mates and supporters alike as he bids a fond farewell to the RDS Arena

(4) Adiós Jordi. Hasta que nos encontremos de nuevo. Jordi Murphy says his own goodbye

1

(1) The Final Act. A journey that began on the
2nd September 2017 in Rodney Parade
concludes on the 26th May 2018 in the
Aviva Stadium. Isa Nacewa and Ken Owens
lead out their teams one last time

(2) Devin Toner defying the laws of gravity and
just about everything else in between
to take this ball under control. Rhys Ruddock
and James Ryan working hard below to keep
the Meath man safe, while James Lowe
can't quite believe his eyes

2

"It's a job well done. 55 players took us to this moment. To do it here in Dublin is very special. A massive day for the club. But a lot of work goes into making this club tick and making it work. For me to leave the club now, at this time and in this place, is special because there's going to be massive things for the future. When you can't keep up with the Leinster standard, it's time to step away. It's over to them now"

Isa Nacewa sets the scene for the season that was. And the future that lies ahead

(1) Devin Toner last scored a try in September 2012 against the Scarlets. He waited a long time for his chance to pounce on them again and duly delivered Leinster's first try of the Guinness PRO14 Final after 29 minutes

(2) Three tries in three games for James Lowe against the Scarlets and this one just before half time would put Leinster 21-11 ahead

5

6

(3) 11 minutes into the second half Leinster have their third try through Seán Cronin

(4) Jordan Larmour scored some special tries during a memorable first season but this kick and chase will live long in the memory alongside his Ulster and Munster tries

(5) That's that. Jack Conan celebrates with Rob Kearney after crossing for Leinster's fifth and final try of the afternoon

(6) 'We got this Skip.' Isa Nacewa and Cian Healy sit back and enjoy the last few moments of a record breaking season

1

2

(1 & 2) To the victors, the spoils. The record breaking Leinster
Rugby players that won a first ever Guinness PRO14 and
Champions Cup double enjoy their moment on the Aviva Stadium
pitch with two pieces of silverware now for company

1

Throw those curtains wide
One day like this a year would see me right
Throw those curtains wide
One day like this a year would see me right for life

One Day Like This – Elbow

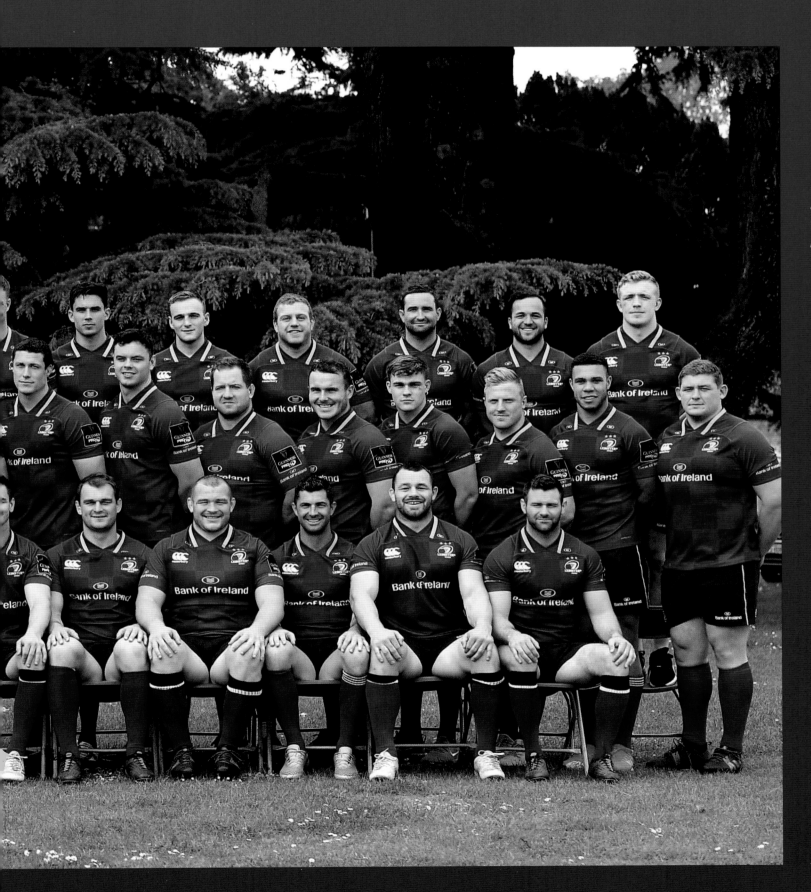

The Leinster Rugby Senior Squad 2017/18 with Leinster Branch President Niall Rynne